architecture 1997 - 2002

published by garlic press august 2002

71 prenton road west. wirral. CH42 9PZ   tel +44 (0) 151 608 7006

designed by shedkm ltd © 2002 printed in barcelona by bookprint SL

ISBN 1-904099-01-7

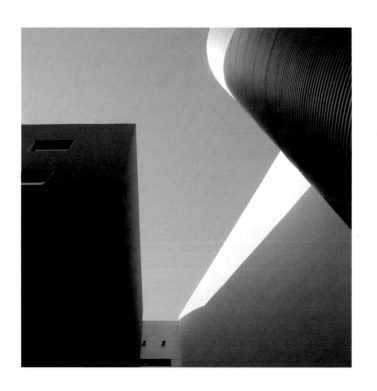

shedkm - a design studio born on a summer afternoon
and grown to a balanced architectural entity in five hectic years.
from obscurity to national award winning status, shedkm's
particular brand of architectural logic has brought together a group
of students and graduates, mainly from liverpool and john moores
universities, into a friendly dedicated studio in liverpool's cultural
ropewalks quarter where graphic designers, actors, poets and
musicians mingle freely with engineers, architects
and new wave developers

shedkm's method is simple - take a problem, expose the parts, put
together a solution based on simplicity, logic and style... more than
this, be enthusiastic - keep to modernist principles and
enjoy being architects

the first five years prove the point - from nothing to a sixteen
strong studio - from no projects to several large completions and
a bookfull of ongoing work. this celebratory publication gives
a glimpse of the result - mainstream modern architecture built
and in use - projects under design and construction -
some dreams and now, many realities...

'nowadays architects are re-discovering the richness of simplicity...'

hans ibelings - 'supermodernism'

ashfield healthcare

ashby de la zouch

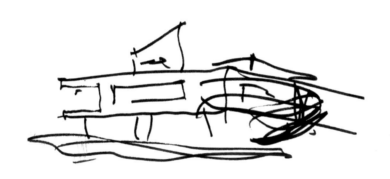

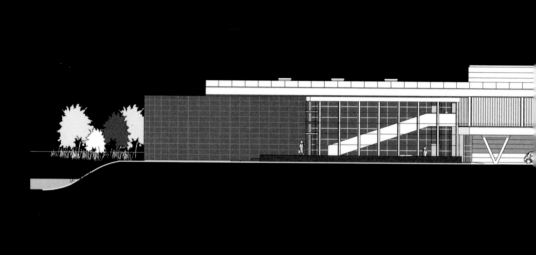

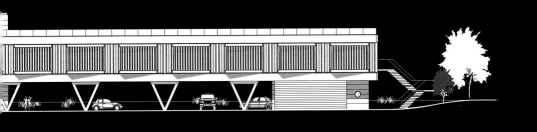

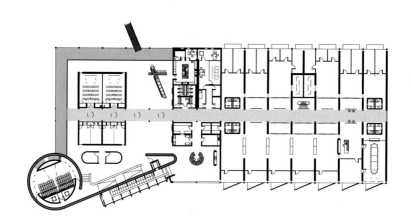

october

november

december

january   february   march   april

sheltered housing
knotty ash. liverpool

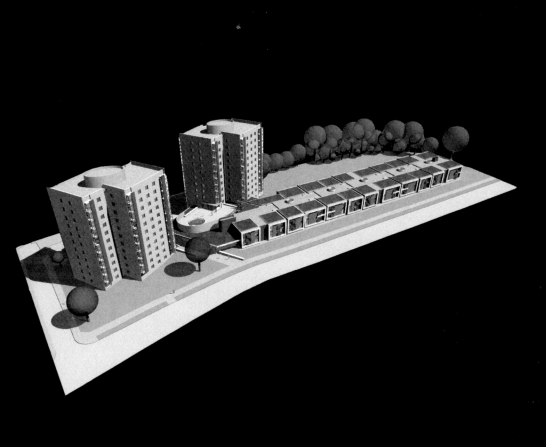

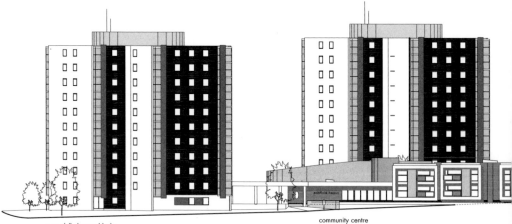

re-modelled tower blocks

community centre

new apartments

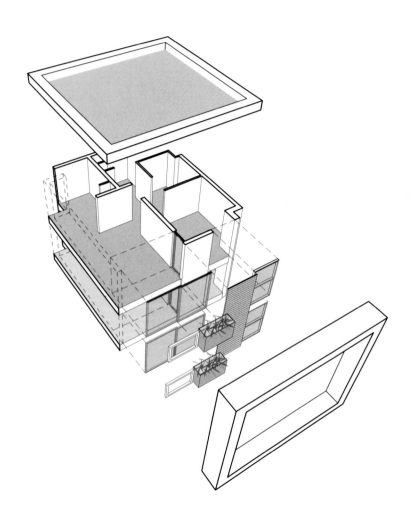

existing

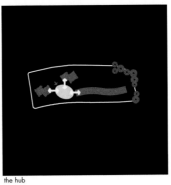

the hub

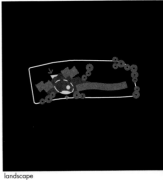

landscape

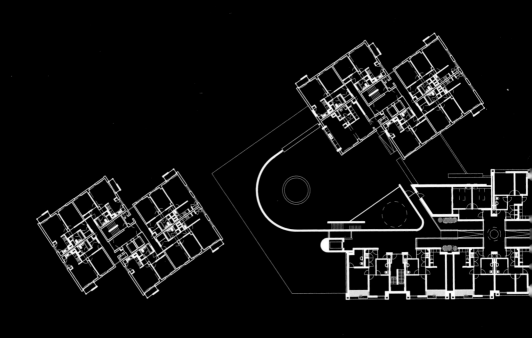

modular apartments
britannia basin. manchester

module

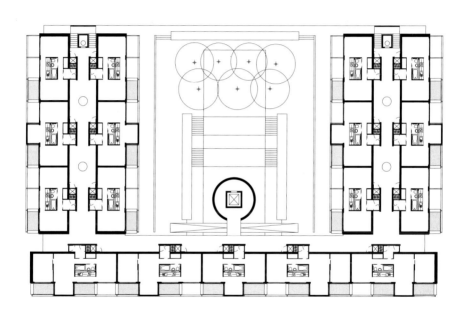

'he who wants to invent has to be capable of reason...'

from an essay by aldo rossi - 1966

the collegiate
shaw street. liverpool

'urban splash and shedkm have played a vital role in kick-starting development in liverpool, bucking economic trends and demonstrating what can be achieved'

alison forrest - prospect journal

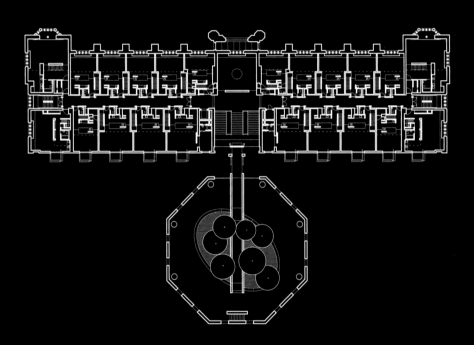

hidden garde

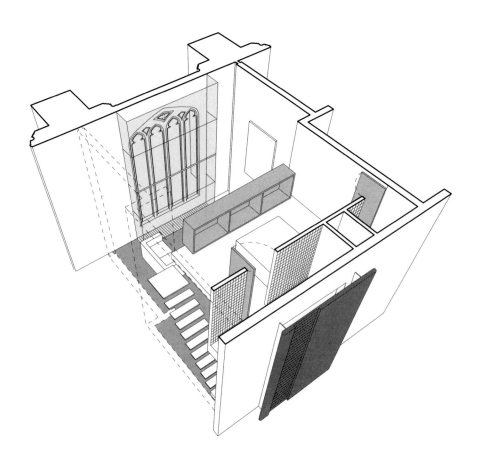

country residence
etwall. south derbyshire

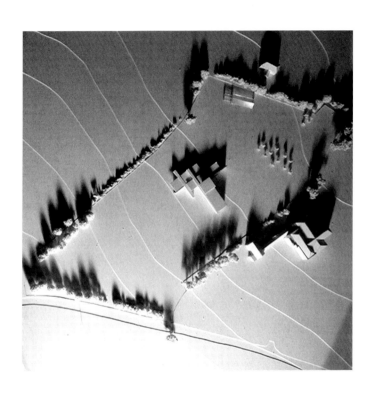

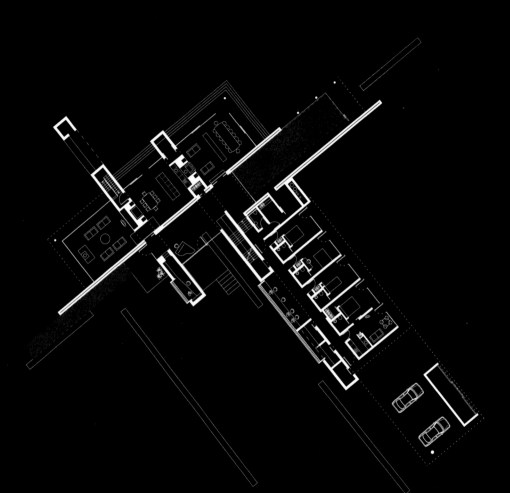

'a desire for well being must be fundamental to all architecture if we are to achieve harmony between the spaces we create and the activities to be undertaken in them...'

jørn utzon - 1948

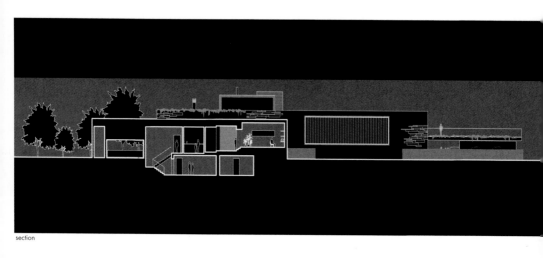

section

del

ski apartment
flaine. france

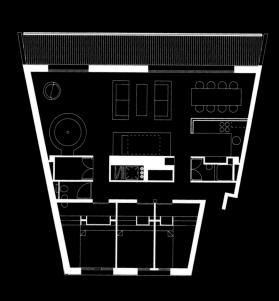

'the valley of flaine in its virgin state was truly remarkable. bright sun and cool breezes were characteristic throughout the entire summer... the air was so clear that distances shrank'

robert f gatje - 'marcel breuer - a memoir'

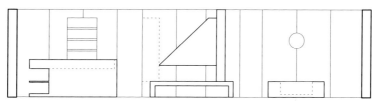

internal elevation

the fort re-generation

fort dunlop. birmingham

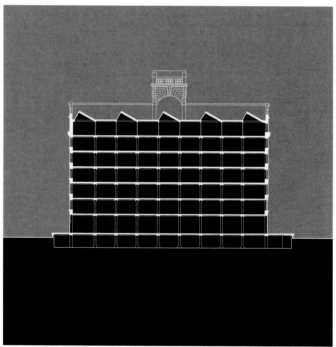

existing

proposed

oak farm houses
allerton. liverpool

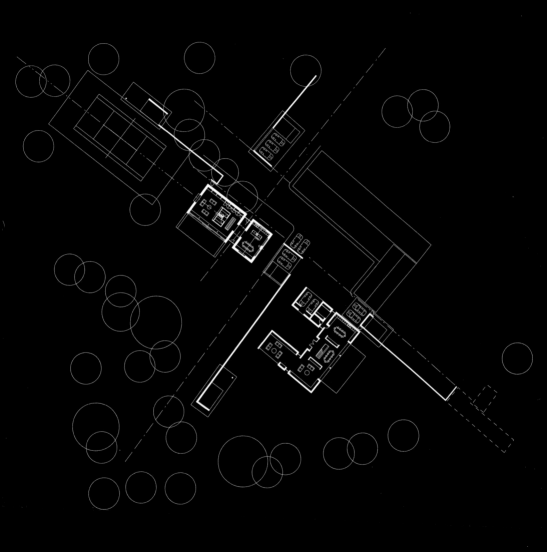

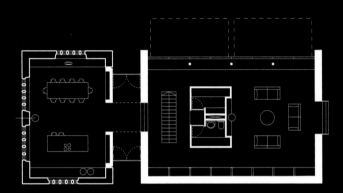

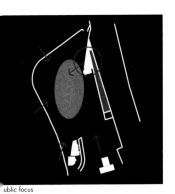

ublic focus

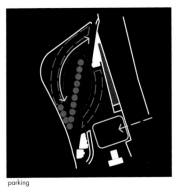

parking

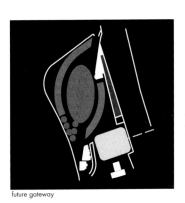

future gateway

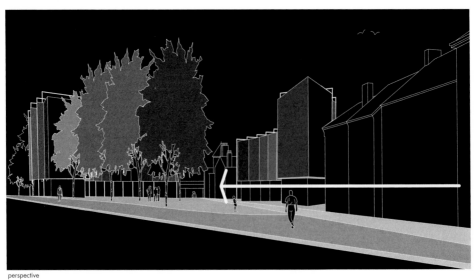

perspective

model

hope on the waterfront
albert dock. liverpool

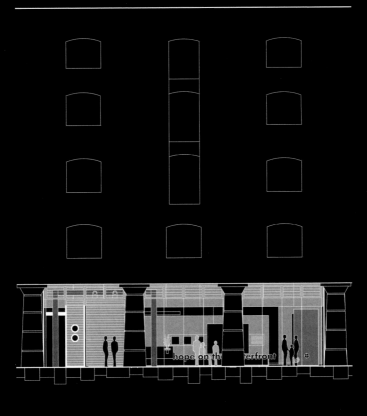

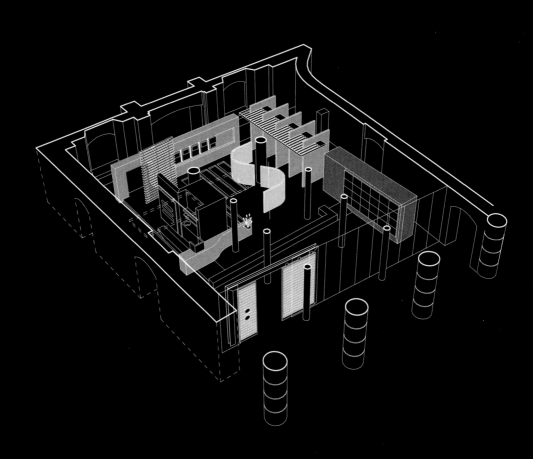

WELCOME TO HOPE ON THE WATERFRONT

house at bidston hill

wirral

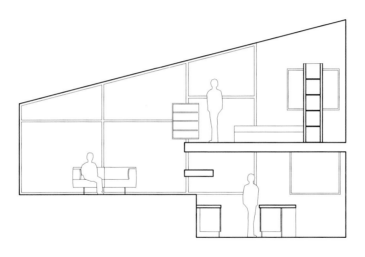

lakeland ltd
windermere. the lake district

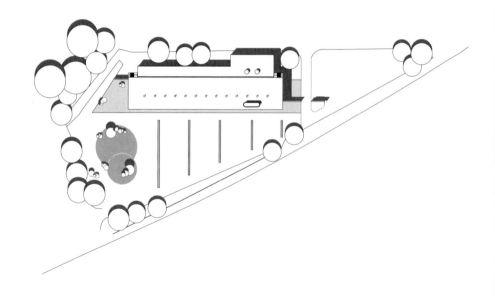

the matchworks
speke garston. liverpool

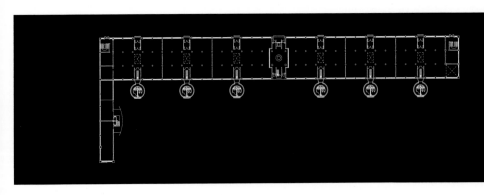

'the clear geometry of the interventions gives them a self-sufficient quality, reminiscent of the hard minimalism of the 1960's artists like judd, morris and andre...'

riba competitions panel

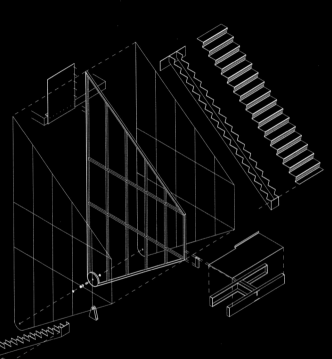

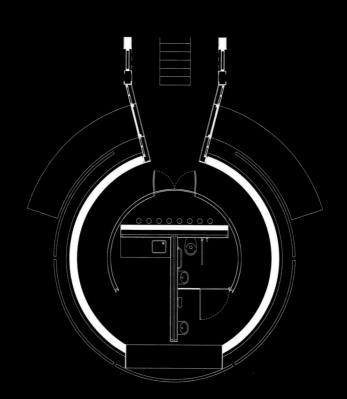

matchbox
speke garston

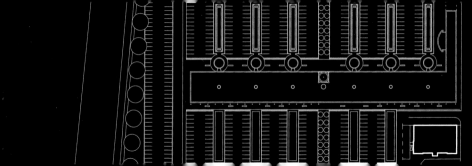

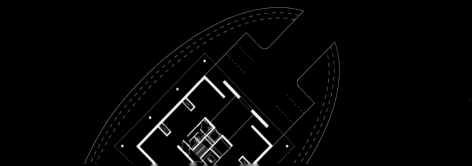

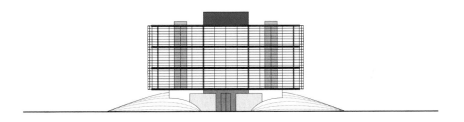

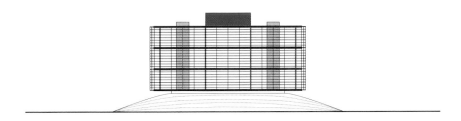

old dye works
oxton. birkenhead

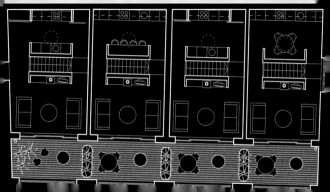

old haymarket
manchester street. liverpool

hotel

new offices

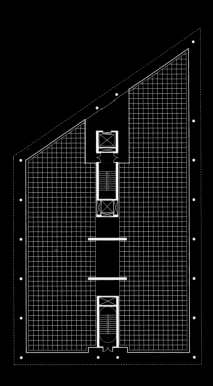

the palace development
wood street. liverpool

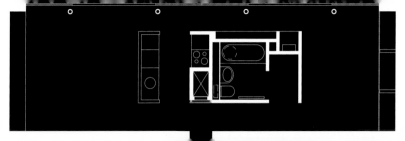

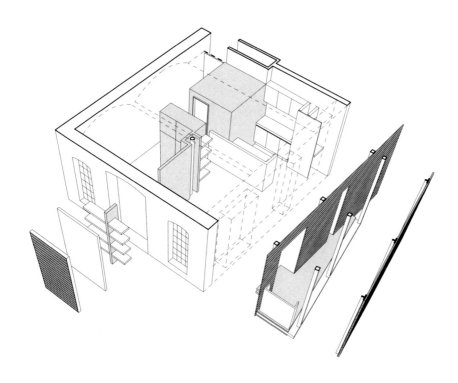

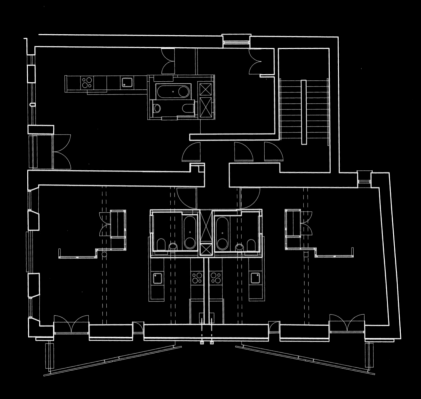

bridge competition
princes dock. liverpool

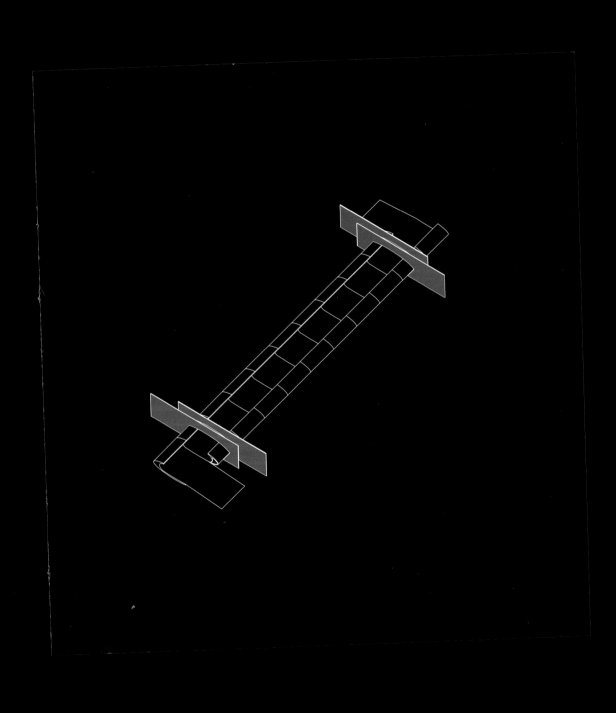

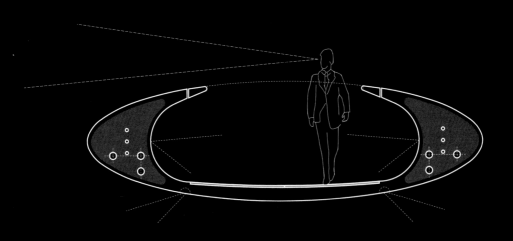

'a clear sky throws up a translucent clearness and after many grim days liverpool assumes a new brilliance. all the colours take on a vibrant freshness and reds stand out with scintillating clarity'

quentin hughes - 'seaport'

psion headquarters
regents park crescent. london

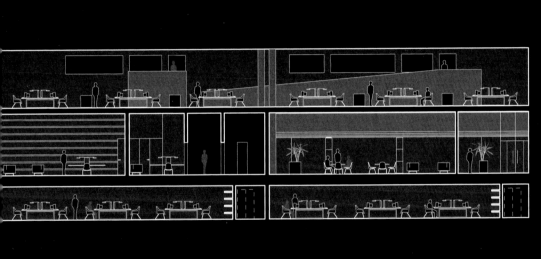

ricci bar-café
bold street. liverpool

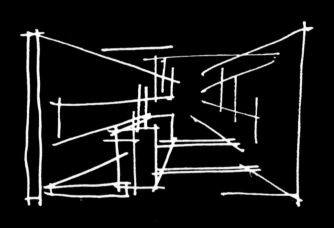

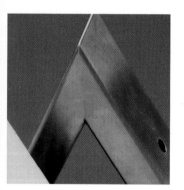

scandinavian hotel
duke street. liverpool

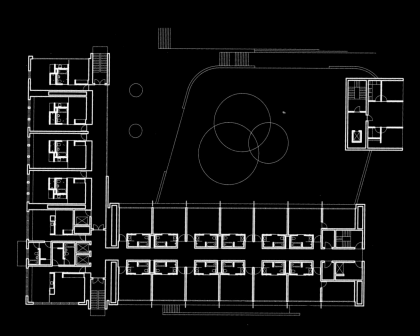

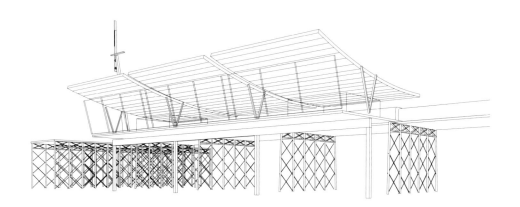

'the architecture of shedkm seems to reflect a native modernist palette of fresh white walls, crisp blues, bright yellow, steel grey, and the transparency of glass...'

dr rob macdonald - liverpool john moores university

st peters church
fleet street. liverpool

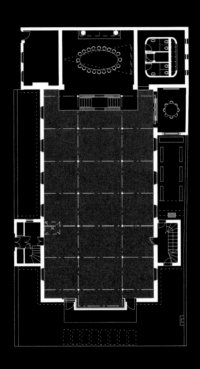

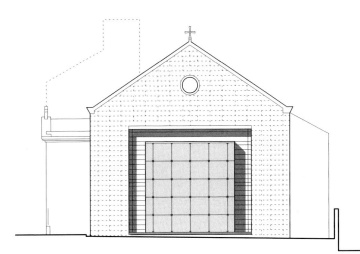

sure start granby
princes avenue. liverpool

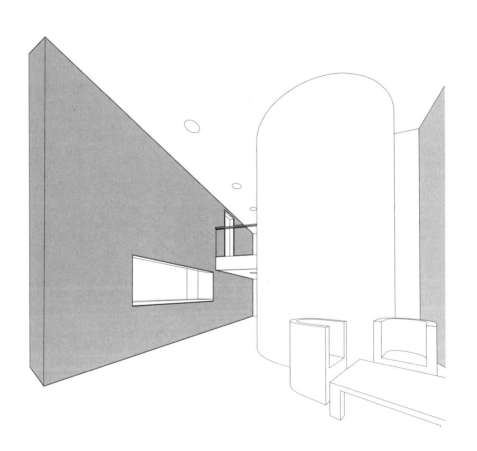

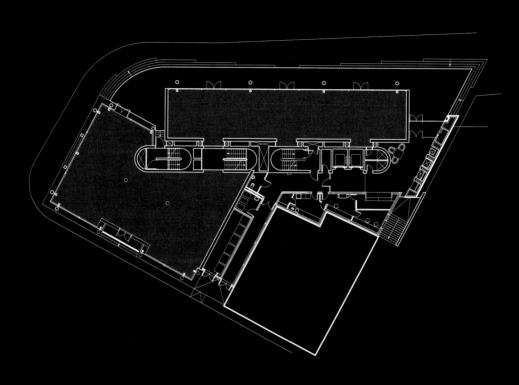

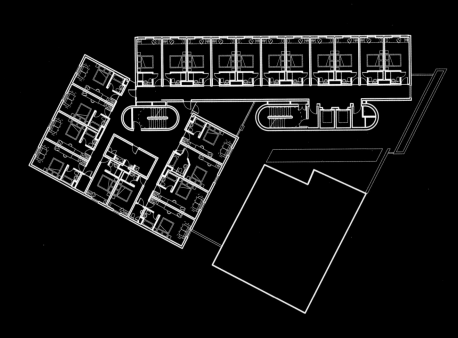

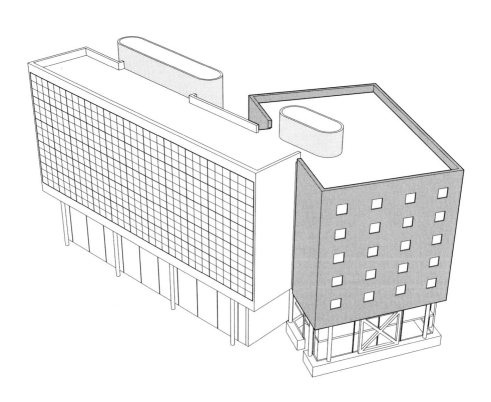

awards

the collegiate

RIBA regional
civic trust national
merseyside civic society
housing design project
liverpool architecture &
design trust

the matchworks

RIBA regional
civic trust national
liverpool architecture &
design trust

preston point

civic trust national
housing design project
housing design final

ricci bar-cafe

merseyside civic society
LDI design

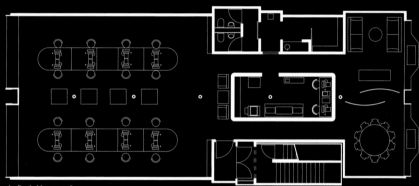

shedkm bold street studio

jon falkingham
james weston
dave king
mark sidebotham
ian killick
hazel rounding
randal turner
dominic wilkinson
rod mcallister (london)
neil dawson
kari simpson
lee halligan
mark braund
barbel gamm
warren mcfadden
stuart dickie
beverly sanderson
ali marshall

miles pearson
niek turner
bettina kasper
alan ross
mark perceval
les ashton
mike jones (london)
amanda wanner
david haselgrove
jonathan fisher
ben johns
quentin keohane
bianka schmitt
guido truffer (geneva)
sophie king o'neill
karen matthews
margaret matthews
ian wylie (london)

thanks are due to

clients: urban splash. wendy dixon, max stone & frenson. maritime housing association. speke garston development company. the liverpool housing action trust. liverpool hope university college. downing developments. giancarlo ricci. bill maynard. sefton metropolitan borough. ed fazakerley & julie barker with compass travelodge. robertson group construction. granby surestart. psion plc. urban splash projects. tom and jo bloxham. urban box ltd. ashfield healthcare ltd. chris and sam corbin. the works trust. bilton ward developments. rod holmes (grosvenor estates). workspace plc. the mandarin. north liverpool partnership. baa bar ltd. hobs ltd. derek matthews. lakeland ltd. sure maintenance. jarvis. paul murphy. the residents of ashgrange/ashfield house. housing 21. direct purpose. henry prescott of mason owen.

consultants: curtins consulting. roy billington associates. whitby bird. buro happold. arup. alan johnston partnership. simon lovell associates. WSP. posford haskonning. steven hunt associates. mcallister landscape. progressive services design. ICS. simon fenton partnership. tweeds. banks wood & partners. stephen davies & associates. capita. baker hollingworth associates. faithfull & gould. c a sothers ltd. splinter. infinite 3D. capture. C3 imaging. ben davies. joule. eric dean. PDW. fulcrum consulting. paul sheen associates. peter gerrard & associates. robert turley associates. english heritage and CABE. ryan-wood. liverpool city, birmingham, south derbyshire, leicestershire and wirral planning, building control and fire officers – thanks also to mcallister co (southport pier). michael jones architects (ashfield healthcare). truffer architectes geneva (flaine), and SJS - ian, george & staff.

also to all of the contractors, subcontractors, suppliers and manufacturers who have made the realisation of shedkm projects possible

photography by

shedkm. jonathan keenan. nick hufton. chris brink. phil sayer and the housing design awards committee

special thanks to angela hurren and guy woodland for help with production and publishing

shedkm

61a bold street. liverpool. L1 4EZ
design@shedkm.co.uk www.shedkm.co.uk

tel +44 (0) 151 709 8211